FLUTE PLAYALONG
CHRISTMAS

WISE PUBLICATIONS
PART OF THE MUSIC SALES GROUP
LONDON / NEW YORK / PARIS / SYDNEY / COPENHAGEN / BERLIN / MADRID / HONG KONG / TOKYO

Published by
WISE PUBLICATIONS
14-15 Berners Street, London W1T 3LJ, UK

Exclusive Distributors:
MUSIC SALES LIMITED
Distribution Centre, Newmarket Road,
Bury St Edmunds, Suffolk IP33 3YB, UK

MUSIC SALES PTY LIMITED
20 Resolution Drive,
Caringbah, NSW 2229, Australia

Order No. AM1001715
ISBN 978-1-84938-719-4
This book © Copyright 2010 Wise Publications,
a division of Music Sales Limited.

Unauthorised reproduction of any part of this
publication by any means including photocopying
is an infringement of copyright.

Engravings and new arrangements supplied by Camden Music.
Backing tracks for 'Here Comes Santa Claus',
'Peace On Earth/Little Drummer Boy'
and 'Walking In The Air' programmed by Danny Gluckstein.
Edited by Lizzie Moore.
CD recorded, mixed and mastered by William Moore.
Cover designed & illustrated by Lizzie Barrand.

Printed in the EU

www.musicsales.com

YOUR GUARANTEE OF QUALITY
As publishers, we strive to produce every book
to the highest commercial standards.
The music has been freshly engraved and the book has
been carefully designed to minimise awkward page turns
and to make playing from it a real pleasure.
Particular care has been given to specifying acid-free,
neutral-sized paper made from pulps which have not been
elemental chlorine bleached. This pulp is from farmed
sustainable forests and was produced with special regard
for the environment.
Throughout, the printing and binding have been planned
to ensure a sturdy, attractive publication which should
give years of enjoyment.
If your copy fails to meet our high standards,
please inform us and we will gladly replace it.

All I Want For Christmas Is You MARIAH CAREY 19

Baby, It's Cold Outside DEAN MARTIN 6

Blue Christmas ELVIS PRESLEY 8

Fairytale Of New York THE POGUES 10

Happy Xmas (War Is Over) JOHN LENNON 12

Have Yourself A Merry Little Christmas FRANK SINATRA 14

Here Comes Santa Claus GENE AUTRY 16
(Right Down Santa Claus Way)

I Believe In Father Christmas GREG LAKE 22

In Dulci Jubilo MIKE OLDFIELD 25

Jingle Bells TRADITIONAL 28

Lonely This Christmas MUD 30

Merry Xmas Everybody SLADE 32

Mistletoe And Wine CLIFF RICHARD 35

Peace On Earth/Little Drummer Boy DAVID BOWIE & BING CROSBY 38

Santa Baby EARTHA KITT 40

Silent Night TRADITIONAL 46

A Spaceman Came Travelling CHRIS DE BURGH 43

Stop The Cavalry JONA LEWIE 48

Walking In The Air ALED JONES 50
(Theme From 'The Snowman')

Wonderful Christmastime PAUL MCCARTNEY 52

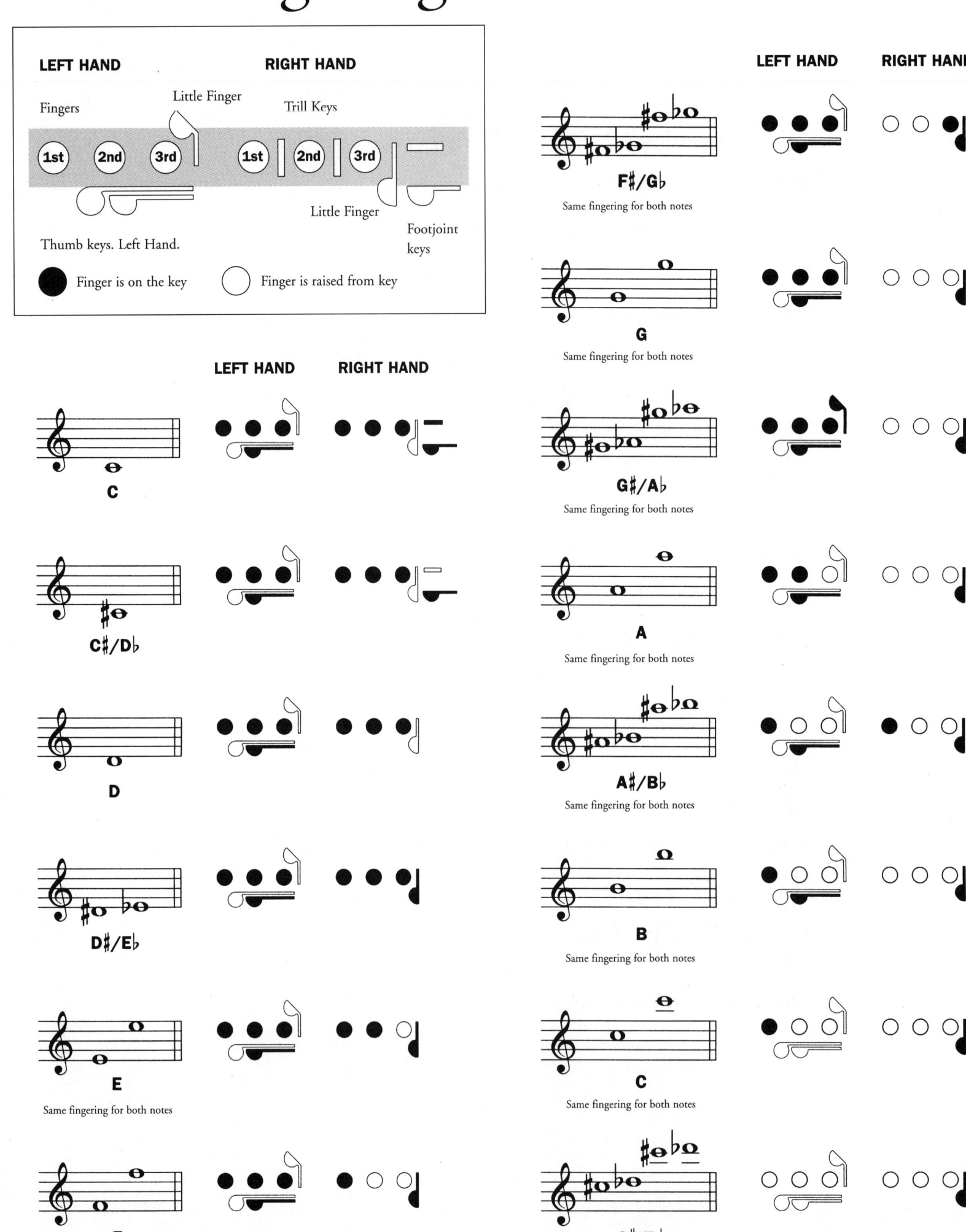

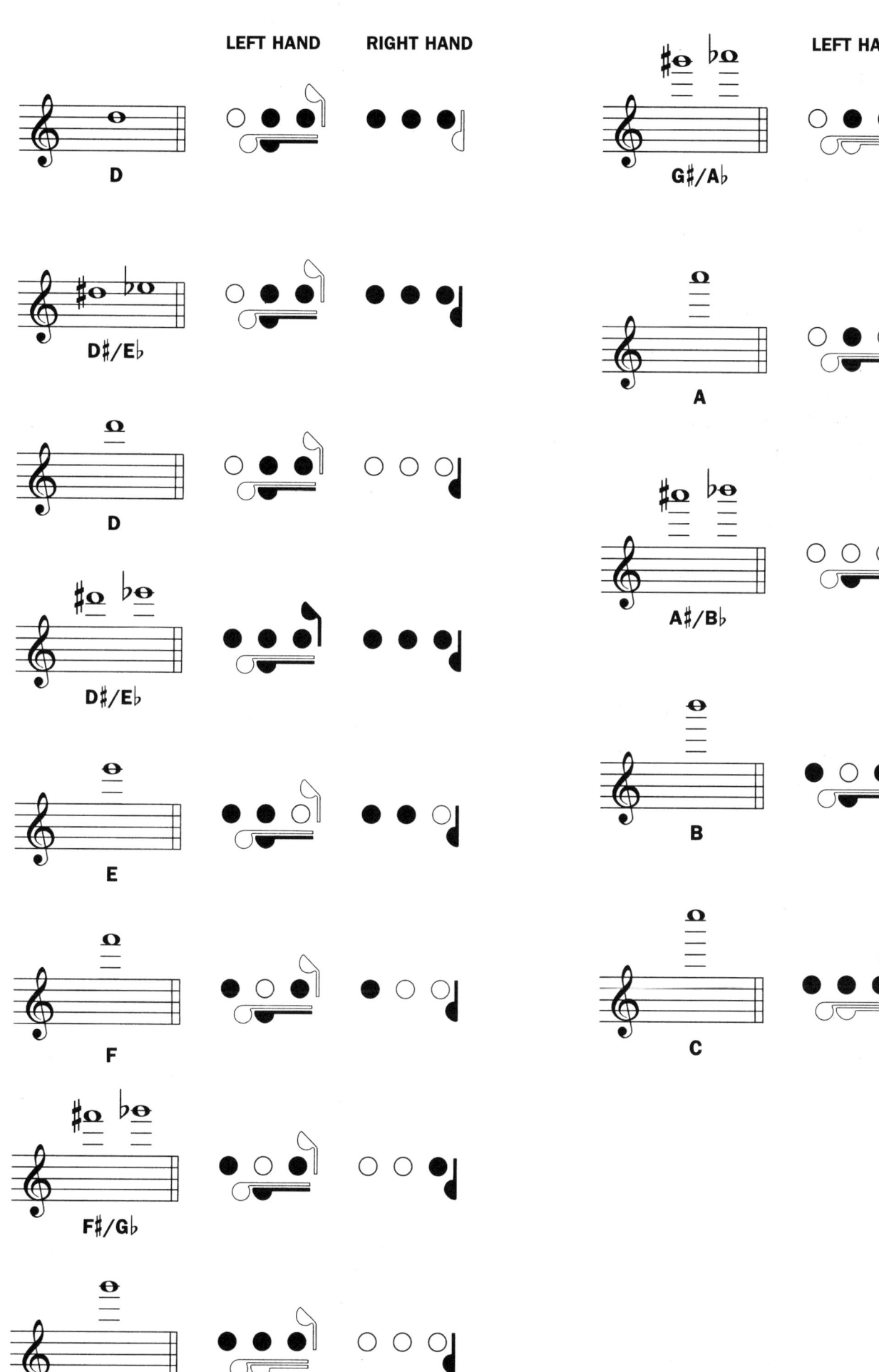

BABY, IT'S COLD OUTSIDE

Words & Music by Frank Loesser

© Copyright 1948 & 1949 (Renewed 1976, 1977) Frank Music Corporation, USA.
MPL Communications Limited.
All Rights Reserved. International Copyright Secured.

Blue Christmas

Words & Music by Billy Hayes & Jay Johnson

© Copyright 1948 Choice Music Incorporated/Bibo Music Publishers Incorporated, USA.
Anglo-Pic Music Company Limited.
All Rights Reserved. International Copyright Secured.

Fairytale Of New York

Words & Music by Shane MacGowan & Jem Finer

© Copyright 1987 Perfect Songs Limited (50%)/Universal Music Publishing MGB Limited (50%)
(administered in Germany by Musik Edition Discoton GmbH, a division of Universal Music Publishing Group).
All Rights Reserved. International Copyright Secured.

Happy Xmas (War Is Over)

Words & Music by John Lennon & Yoko Ono

© Copyright 1971 Lenono Music/Ono Music.
All Rights Reserved. International Copyright Secured.

Have Yourself A Merry Little Christmas

Words & Music by Hugh Martin & Ralph Blane

© Copyright 1944 EMI Feist Catalog Incorporated, USA.
EMI United Partnership Limited, worldwide print rights controlled by Alfred Music Publishing Company Incorporated. Used by permission.
All Rights Reserved. International Copyright Secured.

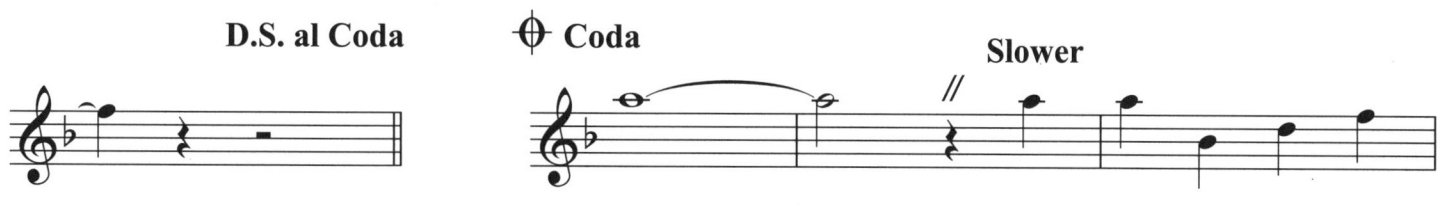
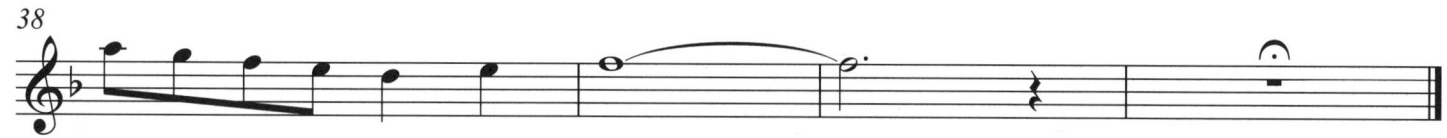

Here Comes Santa Claus
(Right Down Santa Claus Lane)

Words & Music by Gene Autry & Oakley Haldeman

© Copyright 1947 Gene Autry's Western Music Publishing Company, USA.
Campbell Connelly & Company Limited.
All Rights Reserved. International Copyright Secured.

16

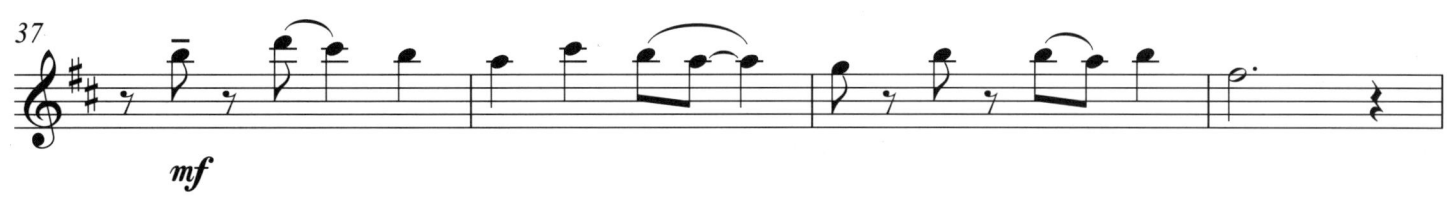

17

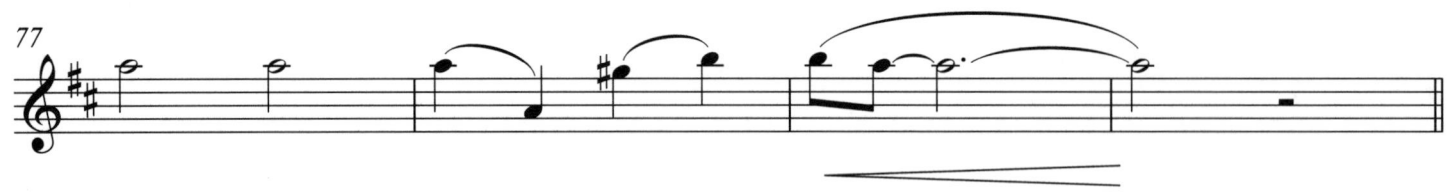
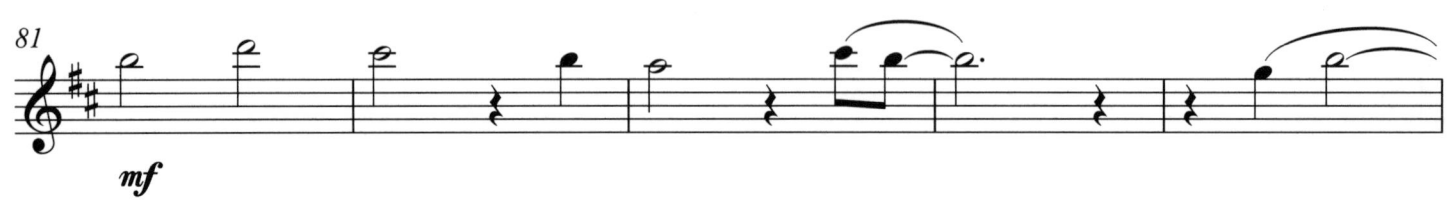

All I Want For Christmas Is You

Words & Music by Mariah Carey & Walter Afanasieff

© Copyright 1994 Rye Songs/Wally World Music, USA.
Sony/ATV Music Publishing (50%)/Universal/MCA Music Limited (50%) (administered in Germany by Universal/MCA Music Publ. GmbH).
All Rights Reserved. International Copyright Secured.

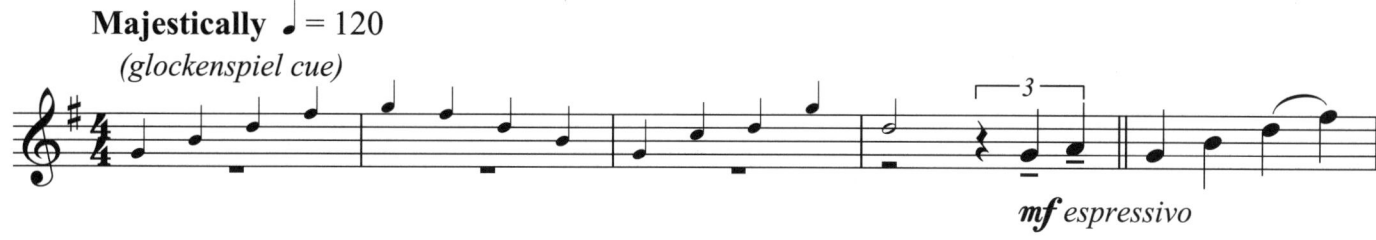

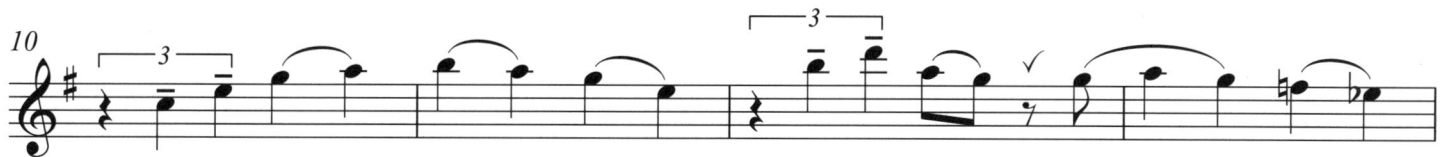

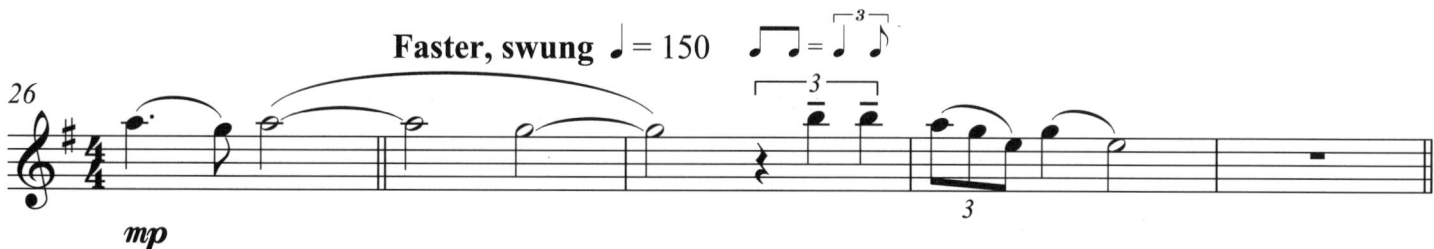

I Believe In Father Christmas

Words & Music by Greg Lake & Peter Sinfield

© Copyright 1975 Leadchoice Limited.
Excerpt from "Lieutenant Kije" by Sergei Prokofiev included by permission of the copyright owners, Boosey & Hawkes Music Publishers Limited.
All Rights Reserved. International Copyright Secured.

In Dulci Jubilo

Traditional

© Copyright 2010 Dorsey Brothers Music Limited.
All Rights Reserved. International Copyright Secured.

25

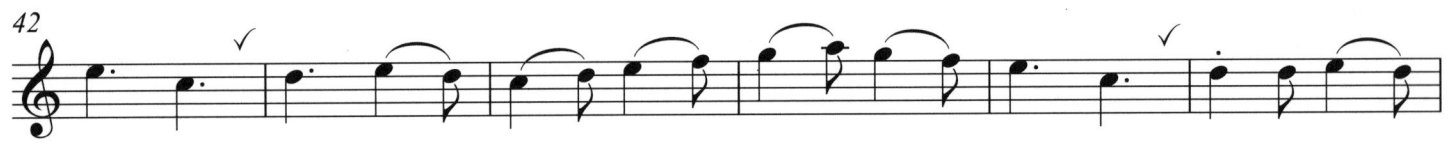

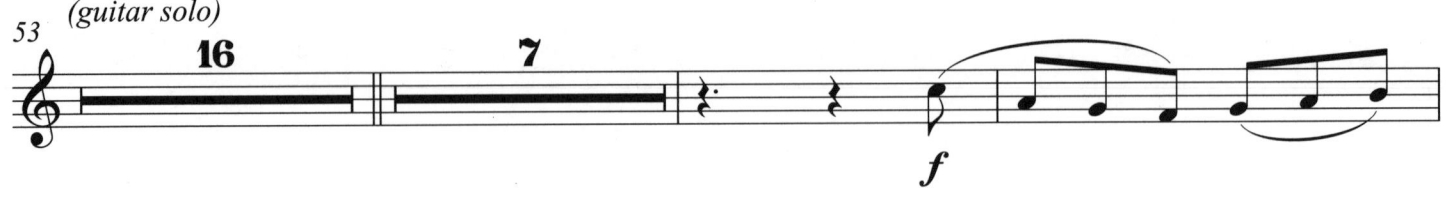

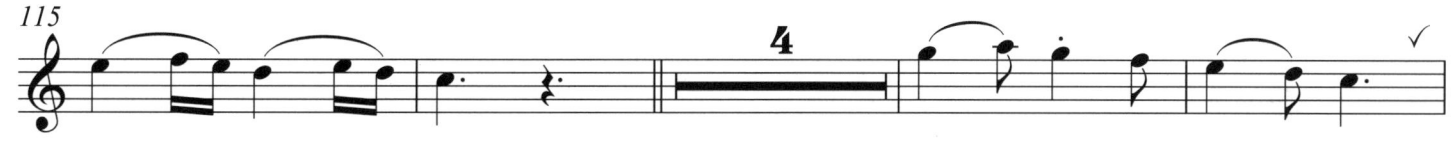

Jingle Bells

Words & Music by James Lord Pierpont

© Copyright 2010 Dorsey Brothers Music Limited.
All Rights Reserved. International Copyright Secured.

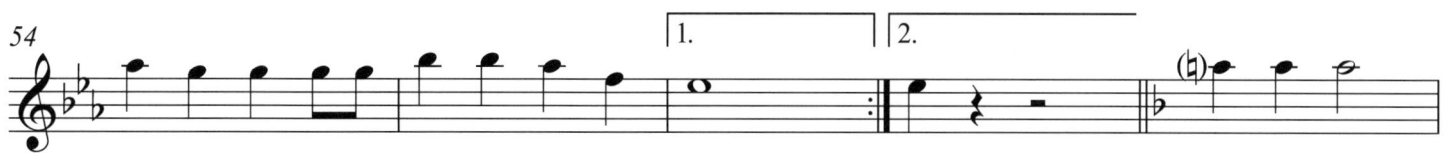
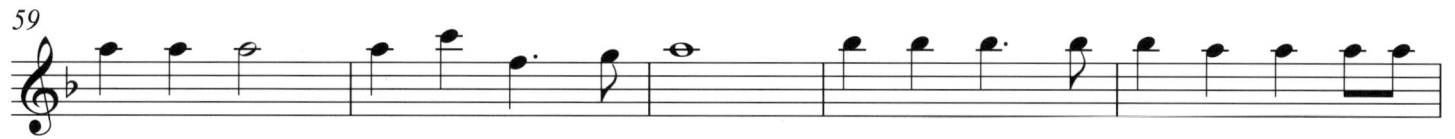

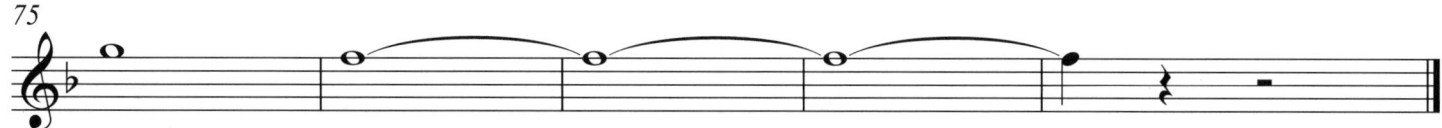

LONELY THIS CHRISTMAS

Words & Music by Nicky Chinn & Mike Chapman

© Copyright 1974 Chinnichap Publishing Limited.
Universal Music Publishing MGB Limited.
All rights in Germany administered by Musik Edition Discoton GmbH (a division of Universal Music Publishing Group).
All Rights Reserved. International Copyright Secured.

Merry Xmas Everybody

Words & Music by Neville Holder & James Lea

© Copyright 1973 Barn Publishing (Slade) Limited.
All Rights Reserved. International Copyright Secured.

Mistletoe And Wine

Words by Leslie Stewart & Jeremy Paul
Music by Keith Strachan

© Copyright 1988 Patch Music Limited.
All Rights Reserved. International Copyright Secured.

35

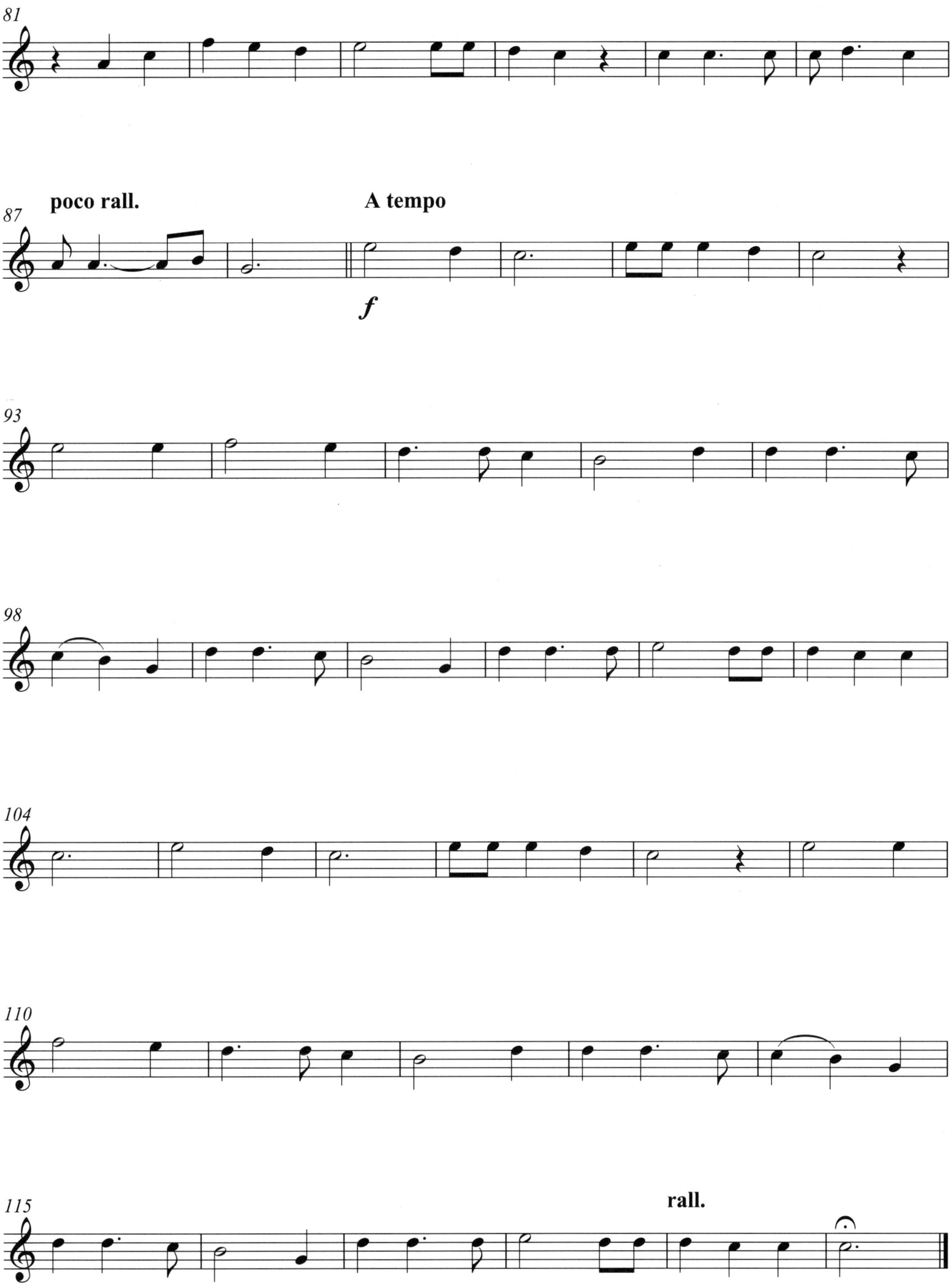
81
poco rall.
87
A tempo
f
93
98
104
110
rall.
115

Peace On Earth/Little Drummer Boy

Peace On Earth
Words by Alan Kohan
Music by Larry Grossman & Ian Fraser

© Copyright 1977 Phraser-Morton Music/One Zee Music, USA.
Chelsea Music Publishing Company Limited (50%)/Warner/Chappell North America Limited (50%).
All Rights Reserved. International Copyright Secured.

Little Drummer Boy
Words & Music by
Harry Simeone, Katherine Davis & Henry Onorati

© Copyright 1958 (Renewed) International Korwin Corporation/EMI Mills Music Incorporated, USA.
Worldwide print rights controlled by Alfred Music Publishing Company Incorporated. Used by permission.
All Rights Reserved. International Copyright Secured.

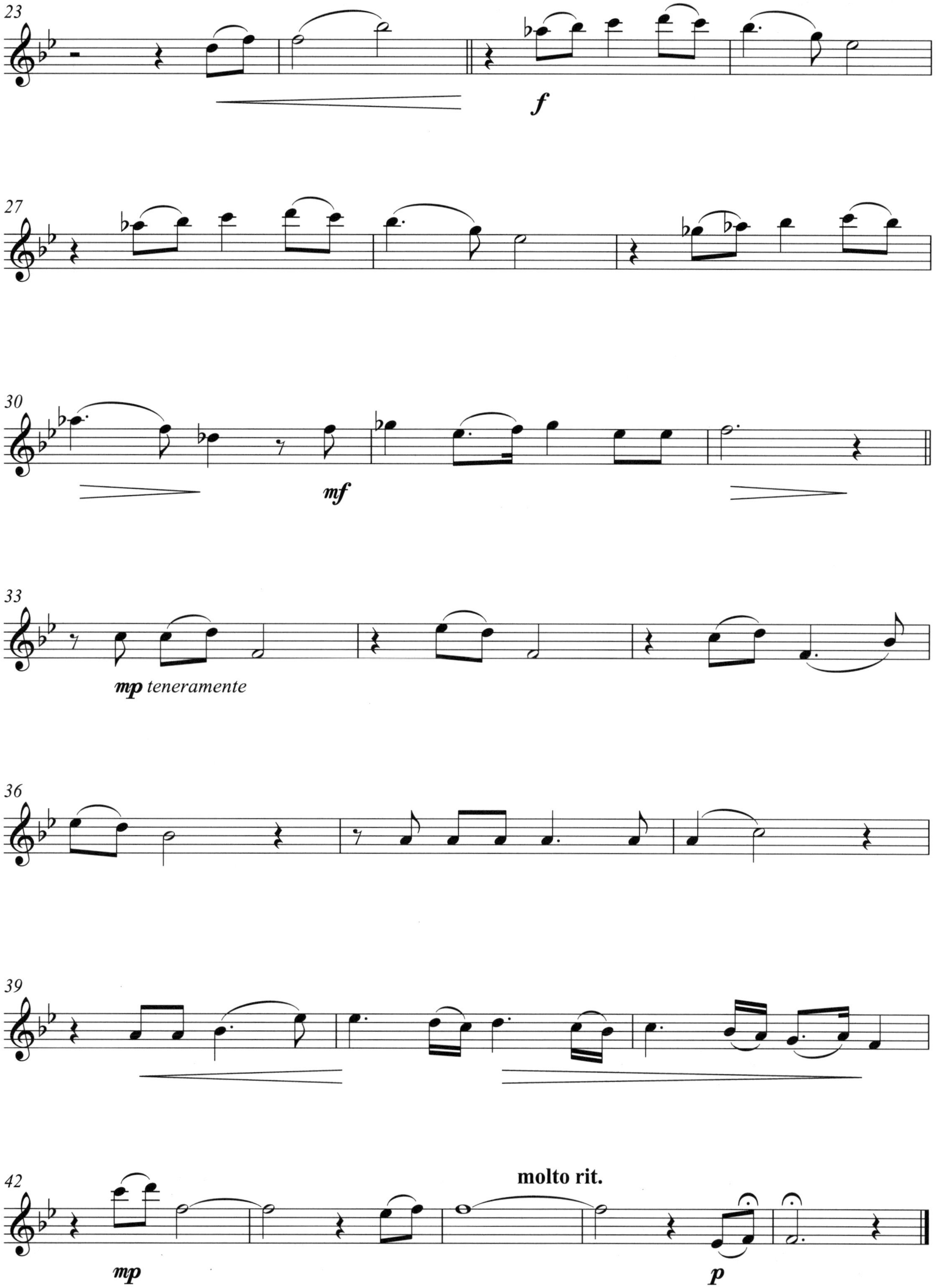
f
mf
mp teneramente
mp
molto rit.
p

Santa Baby

Words & Music by Joan Javits, Phil Springer & Tony Springer

© Copyright 1953 Trinity Music Incorporated, USA.
T.M. Music Limited.
All Rights Reserved. International Copyright Secured.

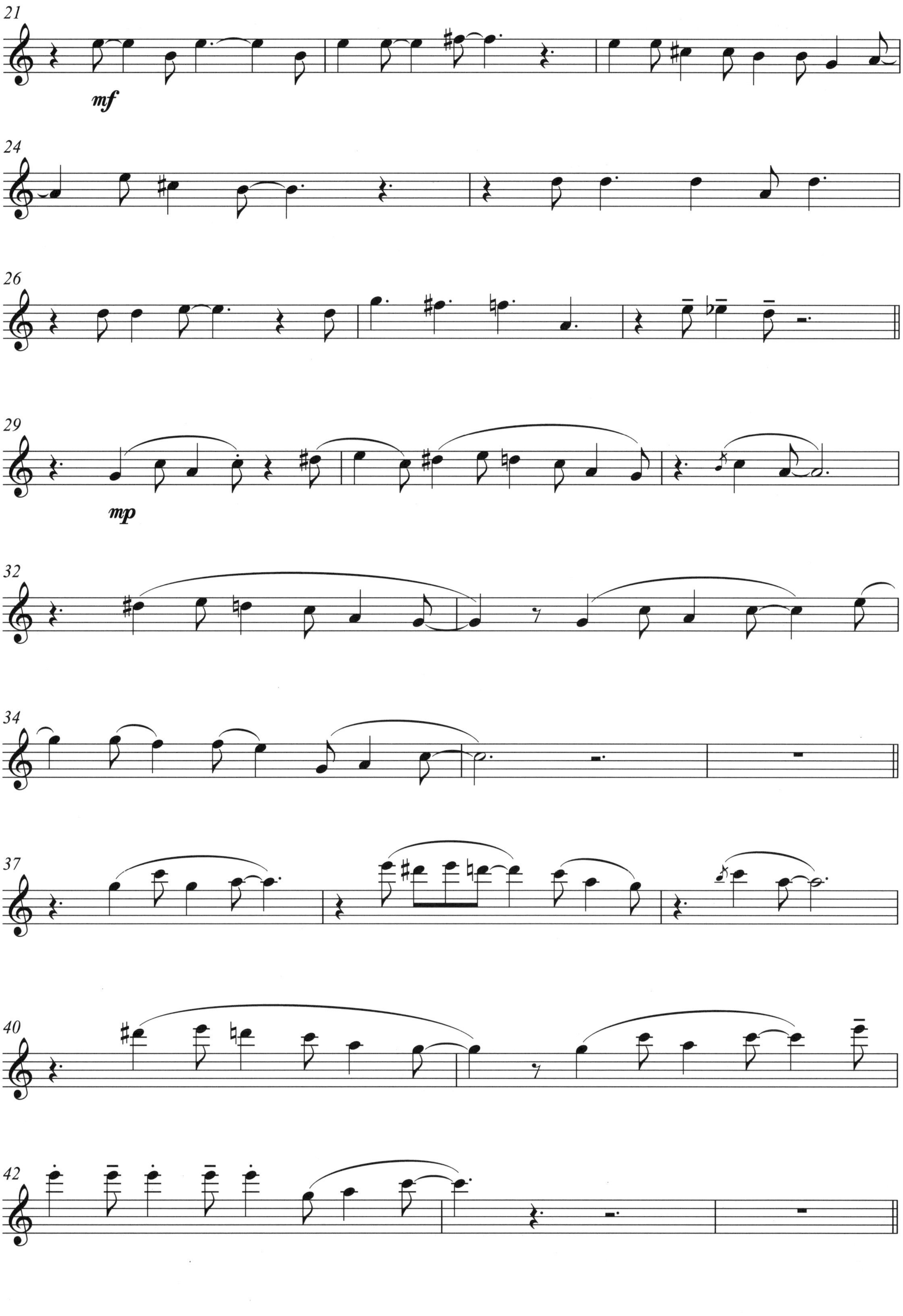
21
mf
24
26
29
mp
32
34
37
40
42

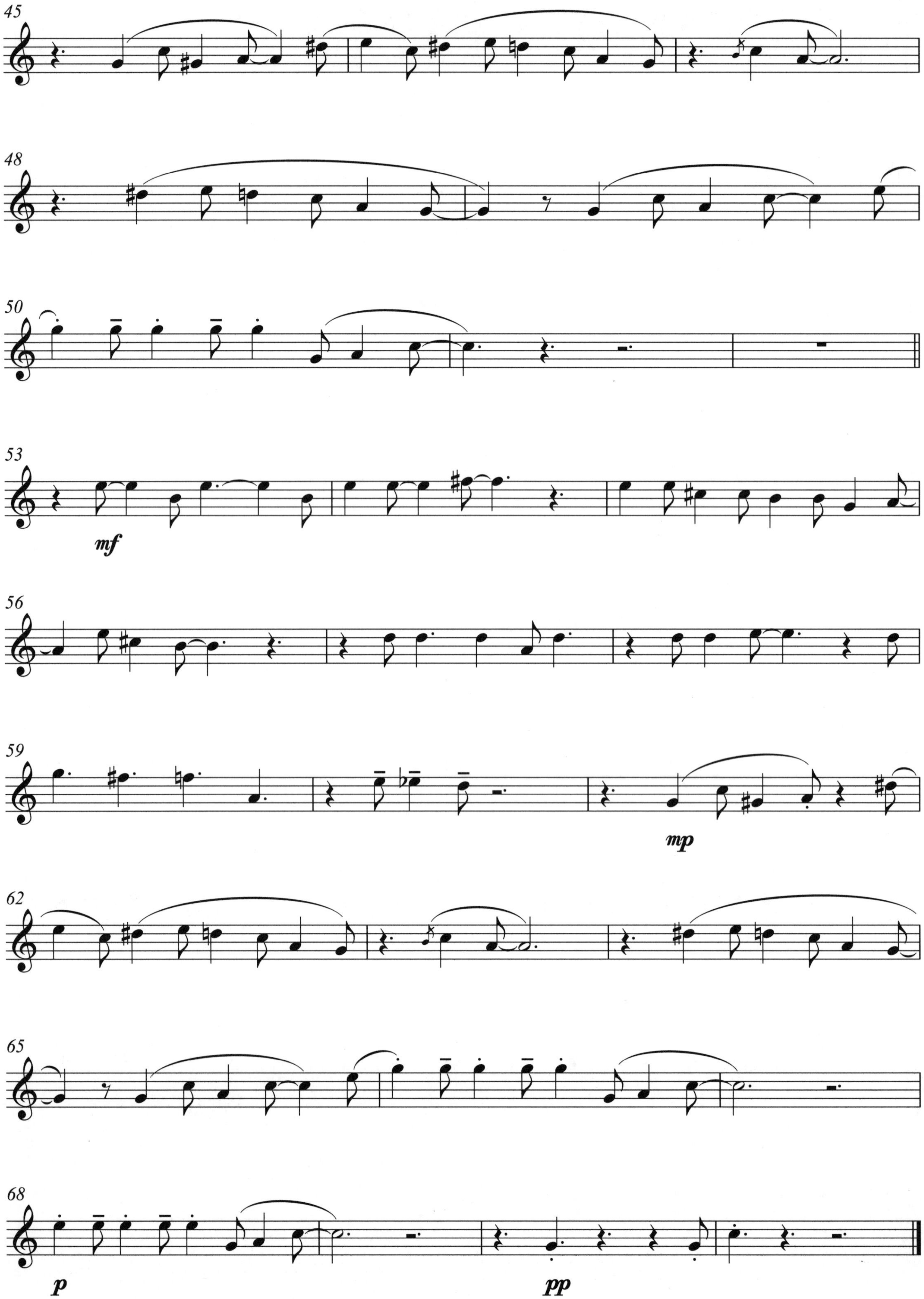
45
48
50
53
mf
56
59
mp
62
65
68
p
pp

A Spaceman Came Travelling

Words & Music by Chris de Burgh

© Copyright 1975 (Renewed 1982) Chrysalis Music Limited.
All Rights Reserved. International Copyright Secured.

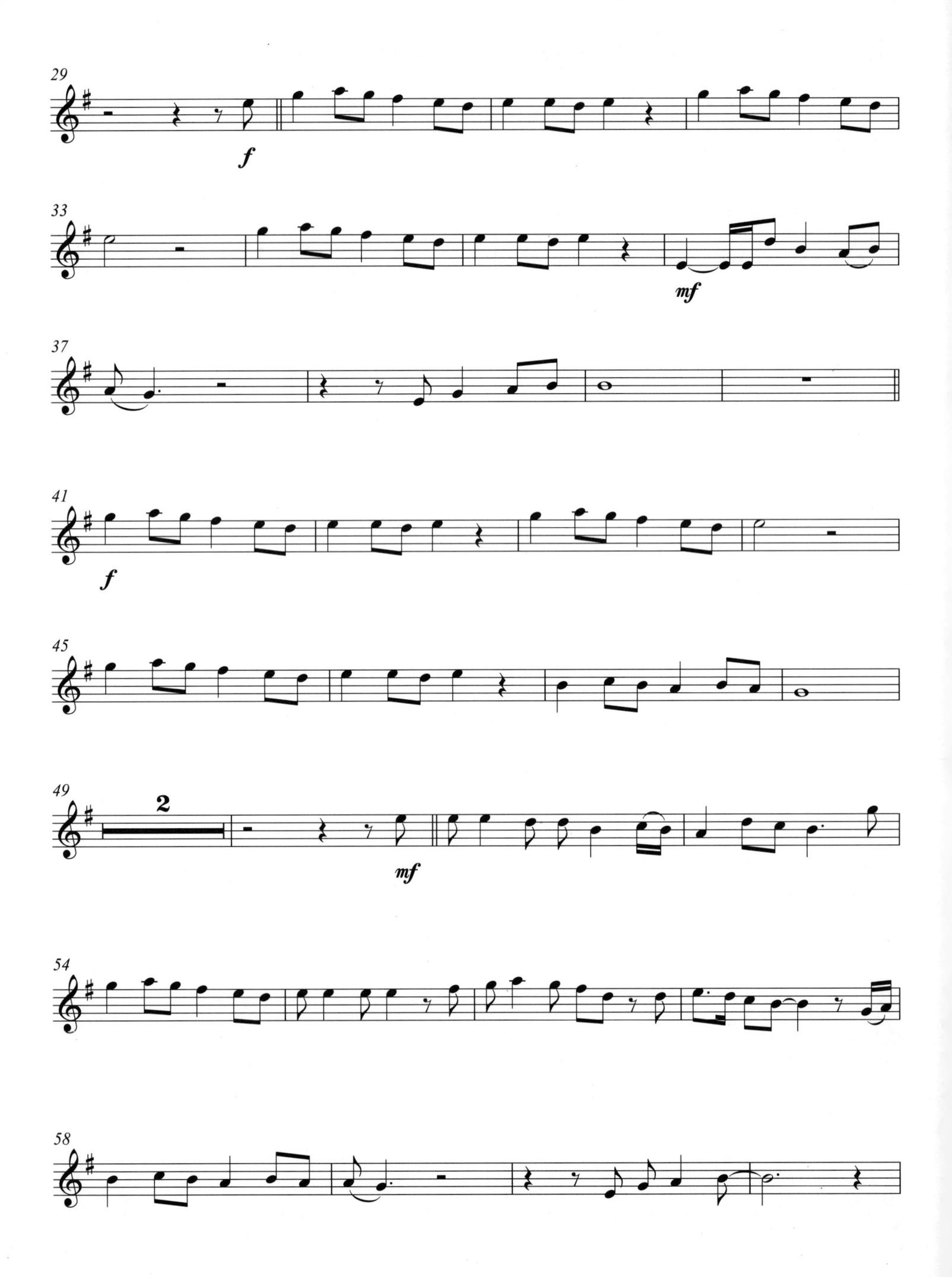
29
f
33
mf
37
41
f
45
49
2
mf
54
58

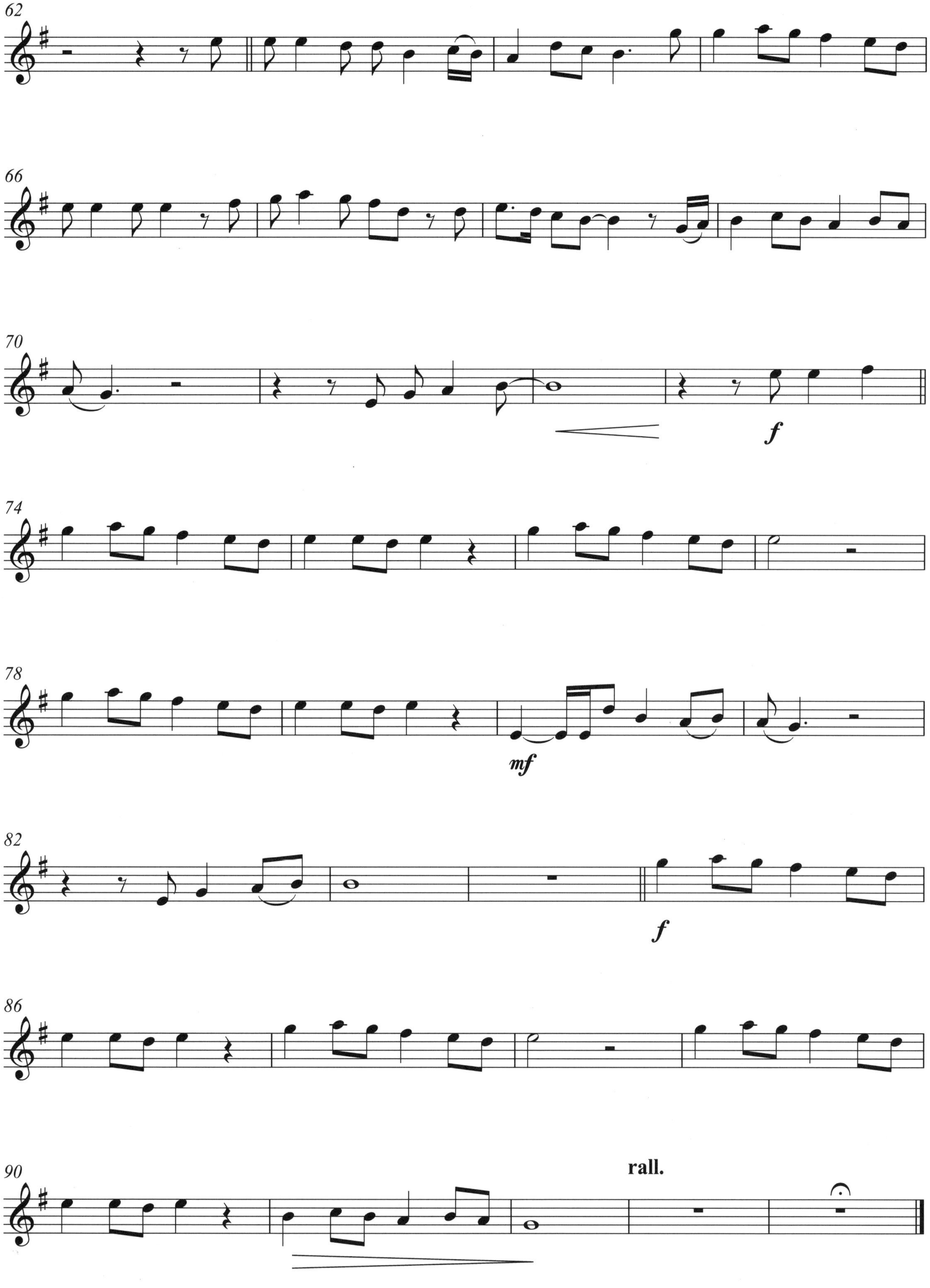
62
66
70
f
74
78
mf
82
f
86
rall.
90

Silent Night

Words by Joseph Mohr
Music by Franz Gruber

© Copyright 2010 Dorsey Brothers Music Limited.
All Rights Reserved. International Copyright Secured.

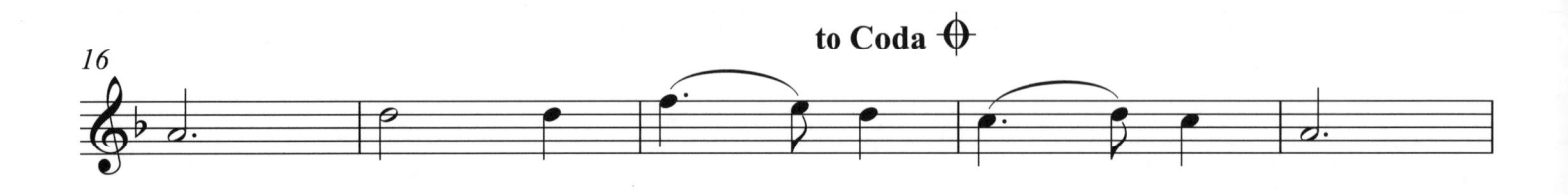

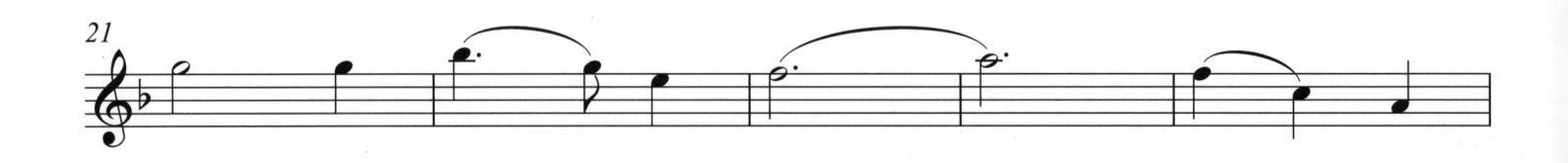

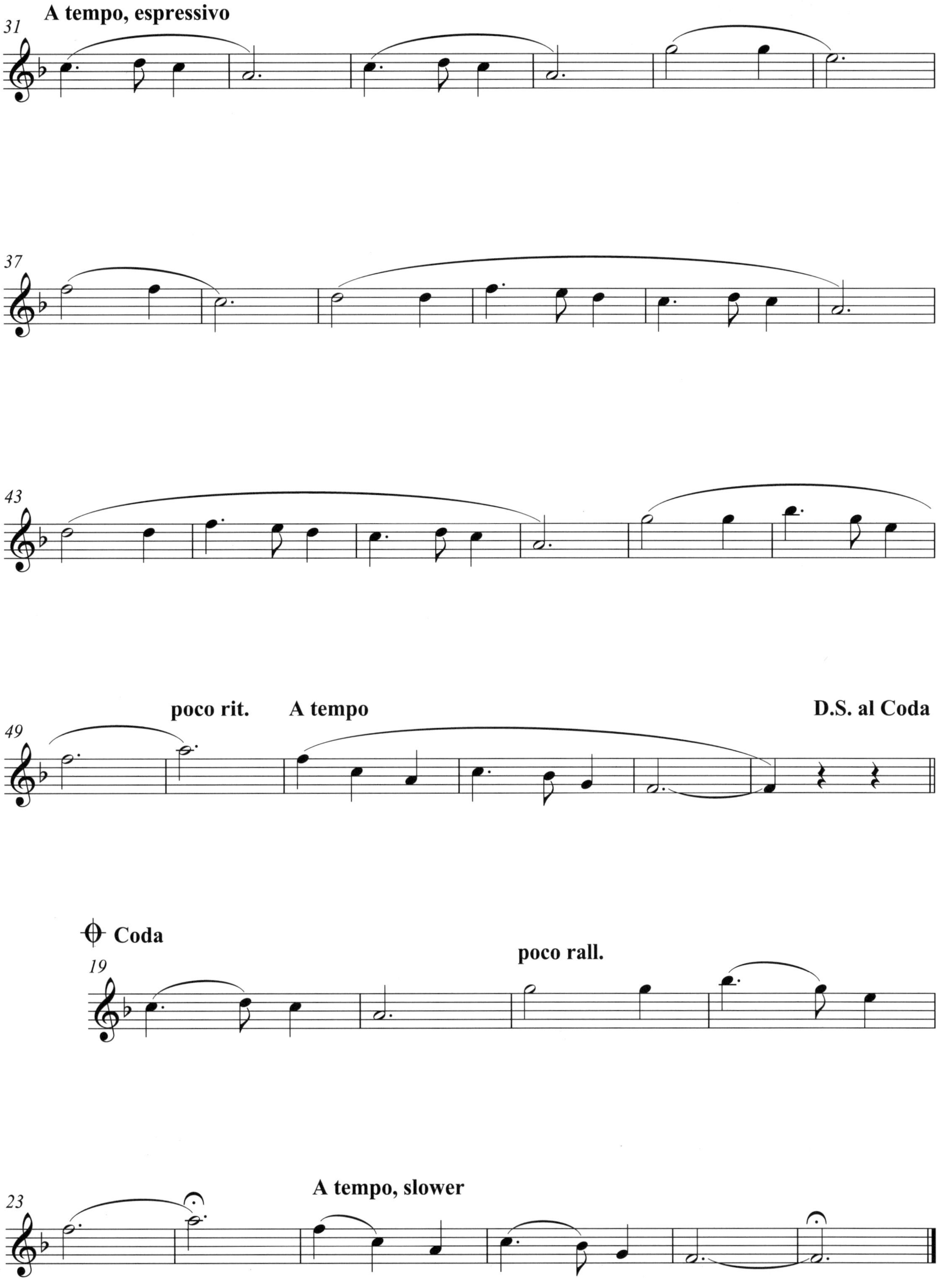
A tempo, espressivo
poco rit.
A tempo
D.S. al Coda
Coda
poco rall.
A tempo, slower

Stop The Cavalry

Words & Music by Jona Lewie

© Copyright 1980 Imagem Songs Limited.
All Rights Reserved. International Copyright Secured.

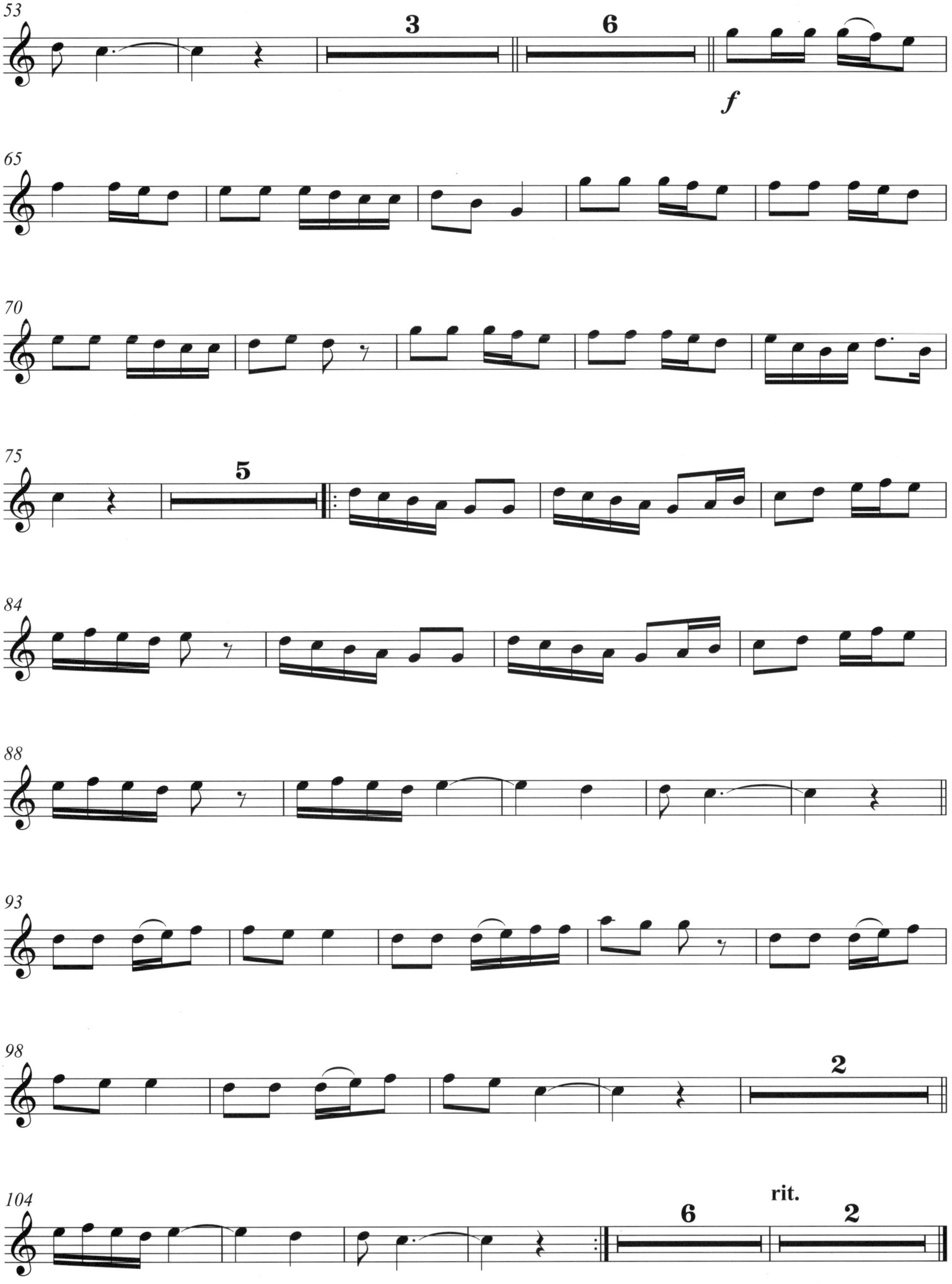
53
3
6
f
65
70
75
5
84
88
93
98
2
104
6
rit.
2

Walking In The Air (Theme from 'The Snowman')

Words & Music by Howard Blake

© Copyright 1982 Highbridge Music Limited.
All rights assigned in 2010 to Chester Music Limited.
© Copyright 2010 Chester Music Limited.
All Rights Reserved. International Copyright Secured.

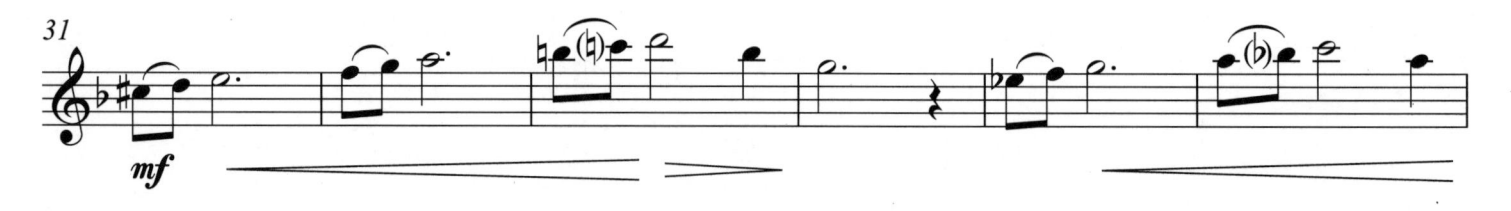

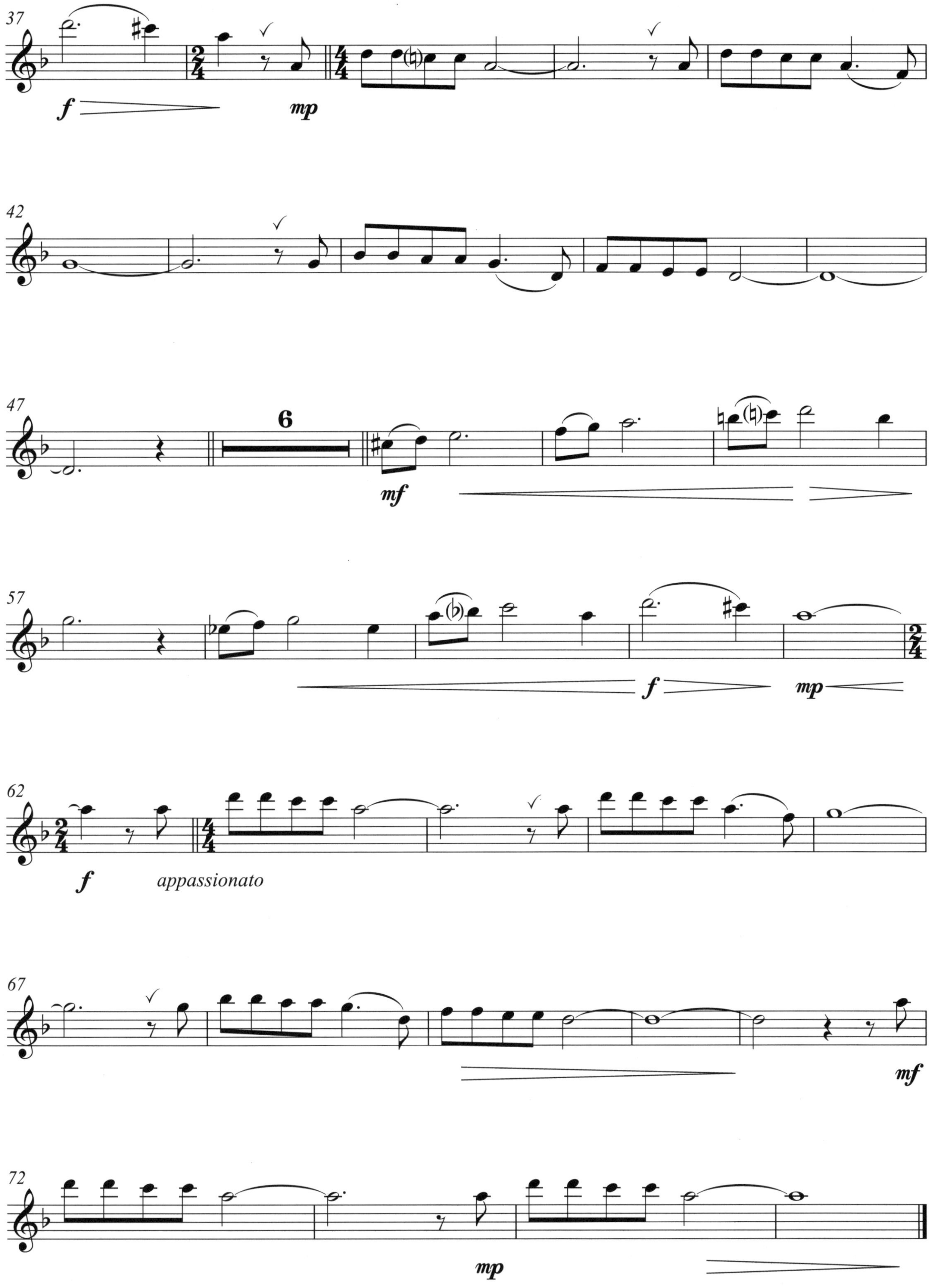
37
f
mp
42
47
6
mf
57
f
mp
62
f
appassionato
67
mf
72
mp

Wonderful Christmastime

Words & Music by Paul McCartney

© Copyright 1979 MPL Communications Limited.
All Rights Reserved. International Copyright Secured.

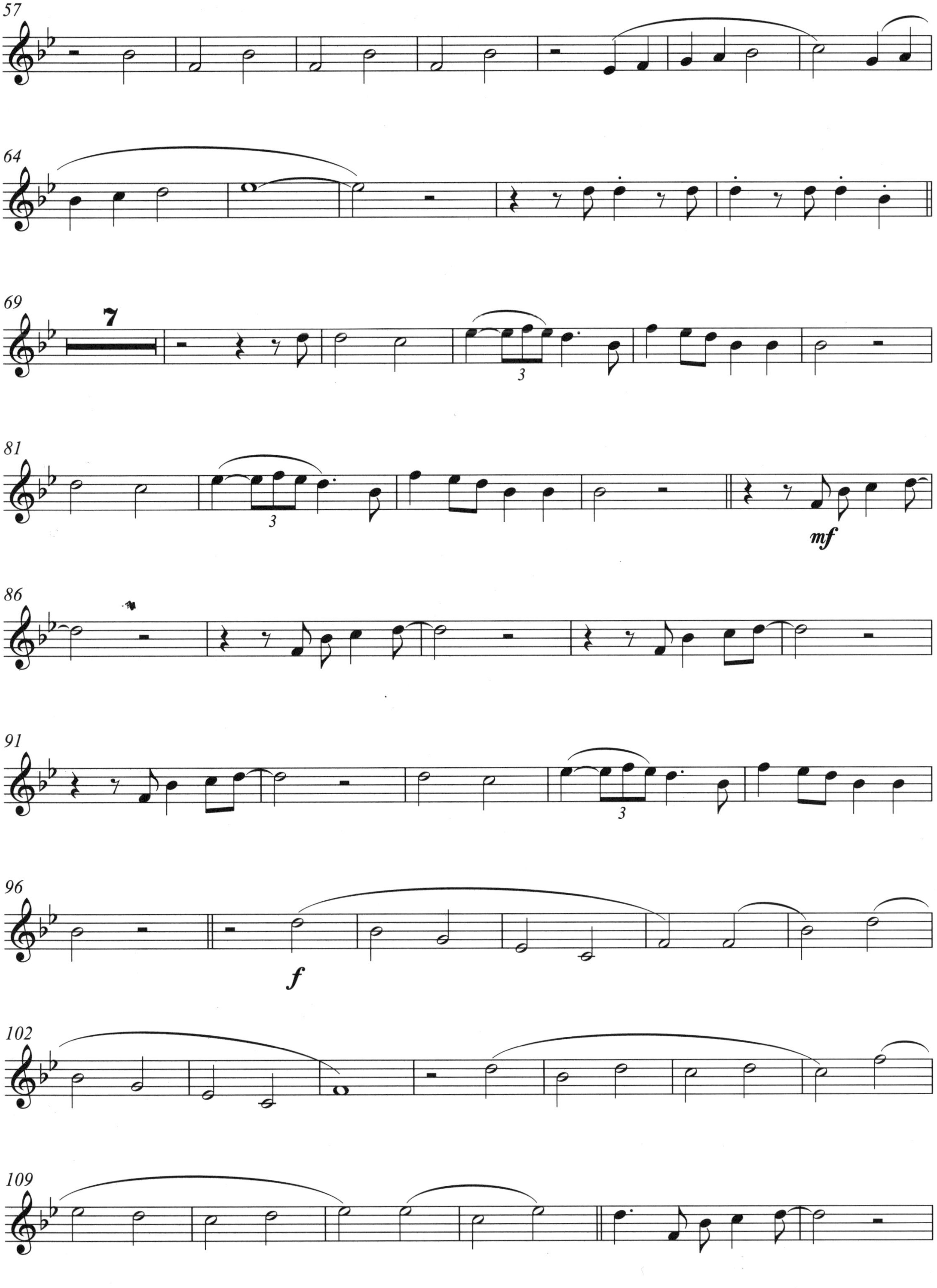
57
64
69
7
81
mf
86
91
96
f
102
109

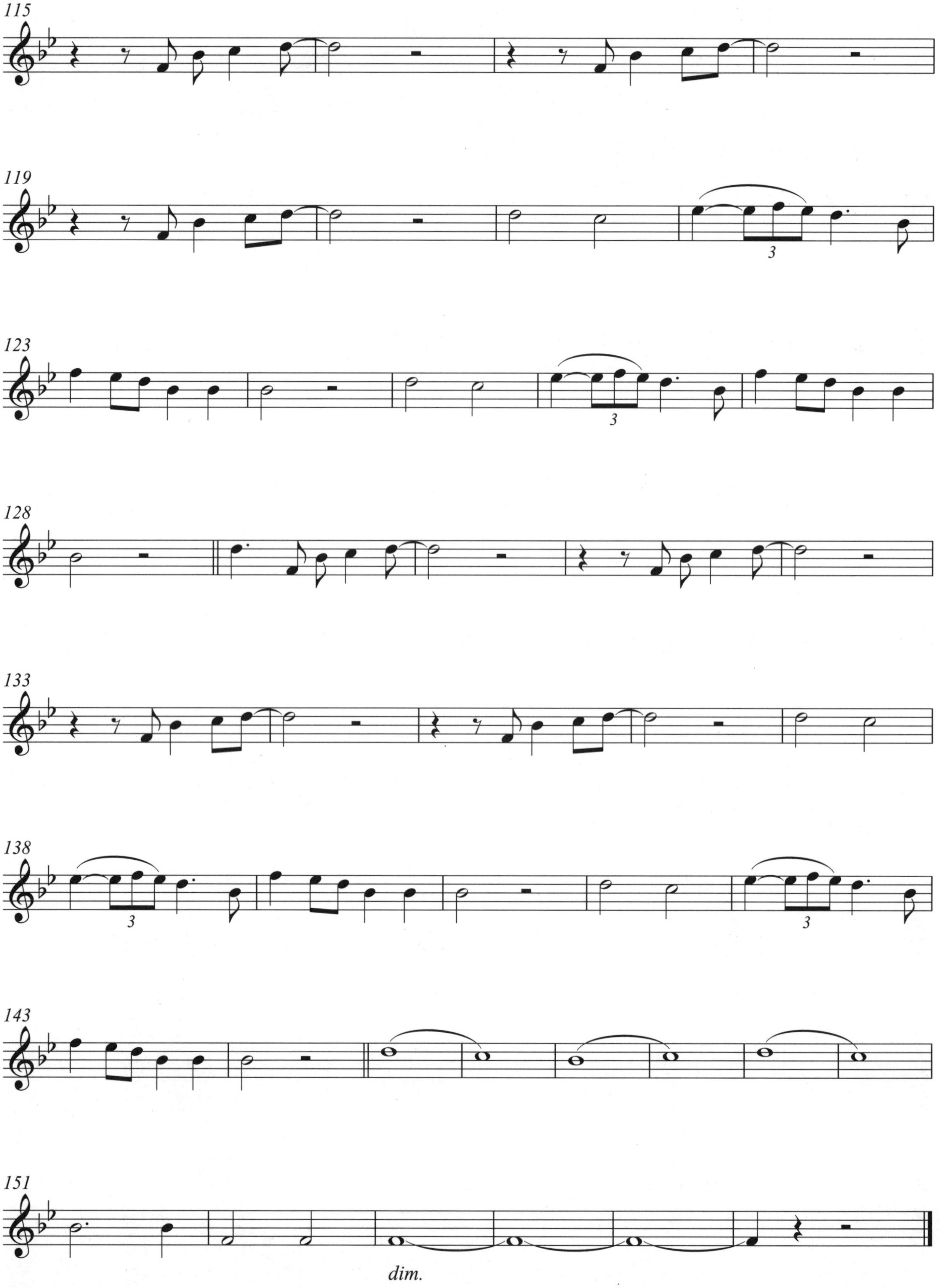

1 2 3 4 5 6 7 8 9

Bringing you the words and the music

All the latest music in print... rock & pop plus jazz, blues, country, classical and the best in West End show scores.

- Books to match your favourite CDs.

- Book-and-CD titles with high quality backing tracks for you to play along to. Now you can play guitar or piano with your favourite artist... or simply sing along!

- Audition songbooks with CD backing tracks for both male and female singers for all those with stars in their eyes.

- Can't read music? No problem, you can still play all the hits with our wide range of chord songbooks.

- Check out our range of instrumental tutorial titles, taking you from novice to expert in no time at all!

- Musical show scores include *The Phantom Of The Opera*, *Les Misérables*, *Mamma Mia* and many more hit productions.

- DVD master classes featuring the techniques of top artists.

Visit your local music shop or, in case of difficulty, contact the Marketing Department, Music Sales Limited, Newmarket Road, Bury St Edmunds, Suffolk, IP33 3YB, UK
marketing@musicsales.co.uk

CD Track Listing

Disc 1

Full performance tracks...

1. Baby, It's Cold Outside
(Loesser) MPL Communications Limited

2. Blue Christmas
(Hayes/Johnson) Anglo-Pic Music Company Limited

3. Fairytale Of New York
(MacGowan/Finer) Perfect Songs Limited/Universal Music Publishing MGB Limited

4. Happy Xmas (War Is Over)
(Lennon/Ono) Lenono Music

5. Have Yourself A Merry Little Christmas
(Martin/Blane) EMI United Partnership Limited

6. Here Comes Santa Claus
(Right Down Santa Claus Way)
(Autry/Haldeman) Campbell Connelly & Company Limited

7. All I Want For Christmas Is You
(Carey/Afanasieff) Sony/ATV Music Publishing/Universal/MCA Music Limited

8. I Believe In Father Christmas
(Lake/Sinfield) Leadchoice Ltd

9. In Dulci Jubilo
(Traditional) Dorsey Brothers Music Limited

10. Jingle Bells
(Pierpont) Dorsey Brothers Music Limited

11. Lonely This Christmas
(Chinn/Chapman) Universal Music Publishing MGB Limited

12. Merry Xmas Everybody
(Holder/Lea) Barn Publishing (Slade) Limited

13. Mistletoe And Wine
(Stewart/Paul/Strachan) Patch Music Limited

14. Peace On Earth/Little Drummer Boy
(Kohan/Grossman/Fraser) Chelsea Music Publishing Company Limited/
Warner/Chappell North America Limited
(Simeone/Davis/Onorati) Warner/Chappell Music Limited

15. Santa Baby
(Javits/Springer/Springer) T.M. Music Limited

16. A Spaceman Came Travelling
(Burgh) Chrysalis Music Limited

17. Silent Night
(Mohr/Gruber) Dorsey Brothers Music Limited

18. Stop The Cavalry
(Lewie) Imagem Songs Limited

19. Walking In The Air
(Theme From 'The Snowman')
(Blake) Chester Music Limited

20. Wonderful Christmastime
(McCartney) MPL Communications Limited

Disc 2

Backing tracks only...

1. Baby, It's Cold Outside

2. Blue Christmas

3. Fairytale Of New York

4. Happy Xmas (War Is Over)

5. Have Yourself A Merry Little Christmas

6. Here Comes Santa Claus
(Right Down Santa Claus Way)

7. All I Want For Christmas Is You

8. I Believe In Father Christmas

9. In Dulci Jubilo

10. Jingle Bells

11. Lonely This Christmas

12. Merry Xmas Everybody

13. Mistletoe And Wine

14. Peace On Earth/Little Drummer Boy

15. Santa Baby

16. A Spaceman Came Travelling

17. Silent Night

18. Stop The Cavalry

19. Walking In The Air
(Theme From 'The Snowman')

20. Wonderful Christmastime